JULY 50 COLORING PAGES
FOR ADULTS RELAXATION

SHIH CHIEN HUA

PUBLISHED BY:
SHIH CHIEN HUA
Copyright © 2018

SEABIRD SHOP >50FOR

FB FAN PAGE

Disclaimer
The information contained in this book is for general information purposes only. The information is provided by the authors and while we endeavor to keep the information up to date and correct, we make no representations or warranties of any kind, express or implied, about the completeness, accuracy, reliability, suitability or availability with respect to the book or the information, products, services, or related graphics contained in the book for any purpose. Any reliance you place on such information is therefore strictly at your own risk.

JULY 1ST

note:

_____

_____

_____

JULY 2ND

note:

_____

_____

_____

JULY 3ND

note:

_____

_____

_____

JULY 4TH

note:

_____

_____

_____

JULY 5TH

note:

_____

_____

_____

JULY 6TH

note:

_____

_____

_____

JULY 7TH

note:

_____

_____

_____

JULY 8TH

note:

_____

_____

_____

JULY 9TH

note:

_____

_____

_____

JULY 10TH

note:

_____

_____

_____

JULY 11TH

note:

_____

_____

_____

JULY 12TH

note:

_____

_____

_____

JULY 13TH

note:

_____

_____

_____

JULY 14TH

note:

_____

_____

_____

JULY 15TH

note:

_____

_____

_____

JULY 16TH

note:

_____

_____

_____

JULY 17TH

note:

_____

_____

_____

JULY 18TH

note:

_____

_____

_____

JULY 19TH

note:

_____

_____

_____

JULY 20TH

note:

_____

_____

_____

JULY 21TH

note:

_____

_____

_____

JULY 22TH

note:

_____

_____

_____

JULY 23TH

note:

_____

_____

_____

JULY 24TH

note:

_____

_____

_____

JULY 25TH

note:

_____

_____

_____

JULY 26TH

note:

_____

_____

_____

JULY 27TH

note:

_____

_____

_____

JULY 28TH

note:

_____

_____

_____

JULY 29TH

note:

_____

_____

_____

JULY 30TH

note:

_____

_____

_____

JULY 31TH

note:

_____

_____

_____

JULY 32TH

note:

_____

_____

_____

JULY 33TH

note:

_____

_____

_____

JULY 34TH

note:

_____

_____

_____

JULY 35TH

note:

_____

_____

_____

JULY 36TH

note:

_____

_____

_____

JULY 37TH

note:

_____

_____

_____

JULY 38TH

note:

_____

_____

_____

JULY 39TH

note:

_____

_____

_____

JULY 40TH

note:

_____

_____

_____

JULY 4TH

note:

_____

_____

_____

JULY 42TH

note:

_____

_____

_____

JULY 43TH

note:

_____

_____

_____

JULY 44TH

note:

_____

_____

_____

JULY 45TH

note:

_____

_____

_____

JULY 46TH

note:

_____

_____

_____

JULY 47TH

note:

_____

_____

_____

JULY 48TH

note:

_____

_____

_____

JULY 49TH

note:

_____

_____

_____

JULY 30TH

note:

_____

_____

_____